DRUMS

HAL LEONARD
Intermediate
BAND METHOD

BY HAROLD W. RUSCH

For class . . . individual . . . full band instruction.

T0112249

PUBLISHED FOR

CONDUCTOR SCORE	Bb CORNET & TRUMPET
C FLUTE	FRENCH HORN in F
OBOE	FRENCH HORN in Eb
Bb CLARINET	Eb MELLOPHONE (ALTO)
Eb ALTO CLARINET	TROMBONE
Bb BASS CLARINET	BARITONE T.C.
BASSOON	BARITONE B.C.
Eb ALTO SAXOPHONE	BBb BASS (TUBA)
Bb TENOR SAXOPHONE	Eb BASS (TUBA)
Eb BARITONE SAXOPHONE	DRUMS

HAL•LEONARD®
CORPORATION
7777 W. BLUEMOUND RD. P.O. BOX 13819 MILWAUKEE, WI 53213

Copyright©1961 HAL LEONARD PUBLISHING CORPORATION
Made in U.S.A.   International Copyright Secured   All Rights Reserved

DRUM ROLL CHART
and RUDIMENTS

Note: The length of any roll to be used is governed by the tempo.
Drums

High Register

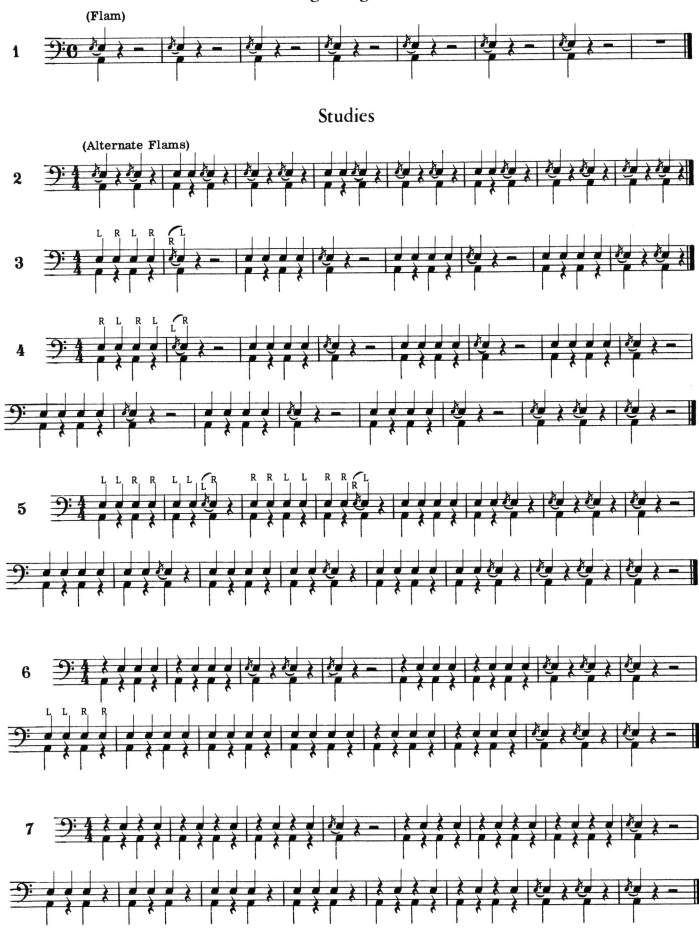

Studies

4

Lightly Row

Folk Song

Harmony

Chord Progressions

Chorale

Exalted Lord

Palestrina

Scale And Intervals

Scale

Studies

Intervals

✪ Refer to roll chart.
Drums

5

Second Symphony

Haydn

(Long roll)

Melody

German
(Long roll)

Harmony
Chord Progressions

Harmony And Rhythm

Chorale
Behold Our Faith Divine

Andantino

Praetorius

Drums

6

Scale

22

Two Octave Scale

23

✱ (Flamacue)

Technical Studies

24

25

26

27

Beneath Thy Guiding Hand

Hatton

28

pp

Folk Song

French

29

mp

✱ Memorize each rudiment.

Drums

Scale

Technical Studies

(Flam accent No. 1)

Staccato And Legato

(Use only wrist action)

⊛ (Single Paradiddle)

Folk Song

Traditional

Melody

Beriot
(adapted)

⊛ Used at this time to teach stick control, and not as a basic rudiment.

Drums

Eighth Notes

38 An eighth note - ♪ - is equal to half of the value of a quarter note - ♩. To simplify reading, whenever two or more eighth notes are written together, the stems are connected by a solid line - ♫ or ♬

An eighth rest - ♪ - is equal to the value of an eighth note.

The lower line contains the number of eighth notes equal in value to the note in the upper line.

The Rhythm Of Eighth Notes

39 The basis of any rhythm is the "Beat." This in turn must be felt as having Two movements, the DOWN ↓ and the UP ↗ . Associate these two movements with the words Sun - Day and Mon - Day . The downward motion coming on the first syllable Sun - ↓ , the upward motion on the second - Day ↗ .

After a feeling for the meter has been established, divide the "Beat" into "1 and"-"2 and".

When learning to play eighth notes, tap the foot in this down and up motion, which is indicated by the arrows ↓ ↗ .

The downward motion comes on the number $\overset{1}{↓}$. The upward motion on the word "and" $\overset{\&}{↗}$.

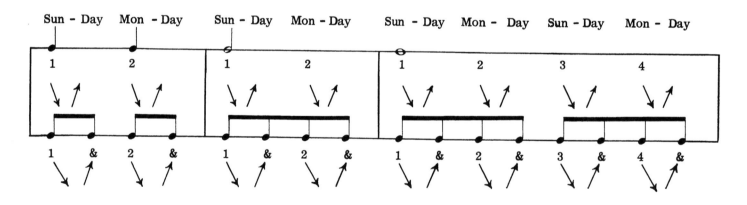

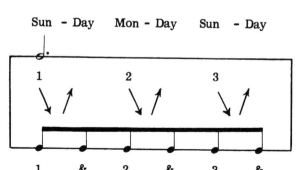

Eighth Note Rhythm Chart

40 **(A)** Chorale read - Tap foot. **(B)** Count and clap - Tap foot. **(C)** Play - Tap foot.
Repeat each rhythm many times.

A Rest may be substituted for any note. The counting remains the same.
All or part of each section may be played together.
✸ **Play on Snare Drum.**

Eighth Notes In 2/4 Time
On The 1st And 2nd Beats

(A) Write the counts under the notes. (B) Play.

On The 1st Beat

(A) Write the counts under the notes. (B) Play.

On The 2nd Beat

(A) Write the counts under the notes. (B) Play.

Studies

First play the studies without the rudiments. After the correct rhythm has been established the rudiments may be added.

(A) Write the counts under the notes. (B) Play.

Fox And Goose

Folk Song

Folk Song

Russian

✱ Refer to corresponding number in the rhythm chart.

Drums

Rhythm Tricks
Upidee

(A) Write the counts under the notes and rests. (B) Play.

College Song (adapted)

Good Night Ladies

(A) Write the counts under the notes and rests. (B) Play.

College Song (adapted)

Eighth Notes In 4/4 Time

One measure of $\frac{4}{4}$ time equals two measures of $\frac{2}{4}$ time.

Studies

(A) Write the counts under the notes. (B) Play.

Robin And His Merry Men

English (adapted)

First Duet

Moderato (Flamacue) (Single Paradiddle)

Shortnin' Bread

Traditional

Allegretto

Drums

12

Rhythm Tricks
She'll Be Comin' Round The Mountain

(A) Write the counts under the notes and rests. (B) Play.

American (adapted)

Eighth Notes In 3/4 Time
Study

(A) Write the counts under the notes. (B) Play.

(S.D.)

Waltz

Czerny

Fine

(Flam accent No. 1)   (B.D. Solo)

D.C. al Fine

Duet

Mozart (adapted)

Moderato   ✲

Rhythm Tricks
Buy A Broom

(A) Write the counts under the notes and rests. (B) Play.

Folk Song

Harmony
Moving Chords

✲ Repeat preceding measure.

Drums

Chorale
Rescue The Perishing

Doane

61 Moderato

Tacet - be silent. (Drum part is omitted.)

Harmony And Rhythm
A Little Man

Humperdinck

Hop, Hop, Hop!

Folk Song

Accompaniment
(May be played with No. 63)

Sea Winds

Thome
(adapted)

Drums

14

The Dotted Quarter Note

A dot after a note increases the value of the note by one half.

Rhythm Chart

66 (A) Chorale read - Tap foot. (B) Count and clap - Tap foot. (C) Play - Tap foot.

A rest may be substituted for any note. The counting remains the same.

On The 1st Beat

(A) Write the counts under the notes. (B) Play.

67

(Snare Drum)

On The 2nd Beat

(A) Write the counts under the notes. (B) Play.

68

(S. D.)

On The 3rd Beat

(A) Write the counts under the notes. (B) Play.

69

(S. D.)

On The 1st And 3rd Beats

(A) Write the counts under the notes. (B) Play.

70

(S. D.)

Two Octave Scale

Technical Studies

In the following studies - Alternate the sticks - Use wrist action - Keep even.
These are preparatory exercises for the strokes of various rolls.

Etude

(The following are accompaniment drumming.)

If necessary write in the counts.

Duet

Hohmann

Moderato

Drums

Santa Lucia

Italian Folk Song

85

Andantino

pp

mf

Playing Independent Parts
The Bell

Traditional

Sixteenth Notes

87 A sixteenth note- ♪ -is equal to half the value of an eighth note- ♪ -or one fourth the value of a quarter note- ♩. Two sixteenth notes equal one eighth note ♪♪=♪, and four sixteenth notes equal one quarter note ♪♪♪♪=♩. To simplify reading, whenever two or more sixteenth notes are written together, the stems are connected by two solid lines- ♬ or ♬♬.

A sixteenth rest- ⅞ -is equal to the value of a sixteenth note, and may be substituted for any one note. The counting remains the same.

The lower staff- C -contains the number of sixteenth notes equal in value to the notes in the upper staves- A or B.

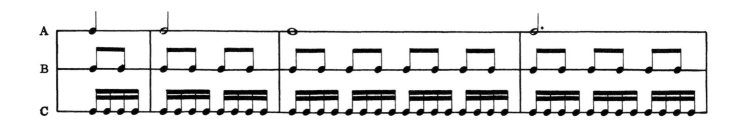

The Rhythm Of Sixteenth Notes

88 Review the "down" and "up" movements of the "beat". Associate these two movements with the words Jan-U-A-Ry and Feb-Ru-A-Ry. The downward motion coming on the first two syllables- Jan-U ↘ ; the upward motion on the last two - A-Ry ↗ . After a feeling for the meter has been established, divide the "beat" into 1-e-&-a, 2-e-&-a- etc. The rhythm of the counting corresponds to the rhythm of the words January and February.

When learning to play sixteenth notes, tap the foot in the down and up motion- 1-e-&-a, 2-e-&-a.

Sixteenth Note Rhythm Chart

89 (A) Chorale read - Tap foot. (B) Count and clap - Tap foot. (C) Play - Tap foot. Repeat each rhythm many times.

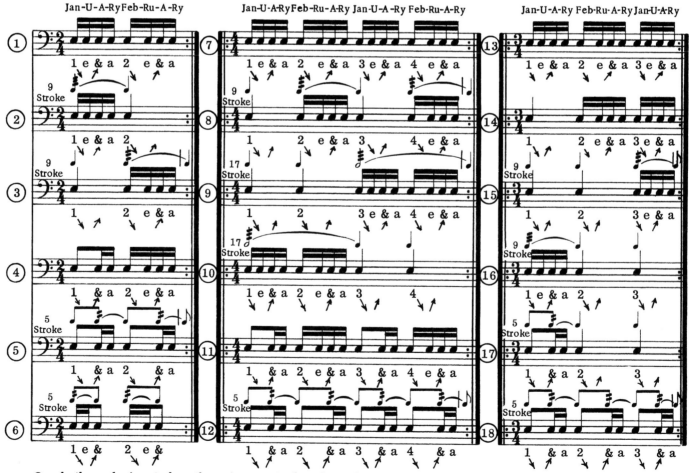

On rhythms designated as the primary strokes for rolls - (1) Play the sixteenth notes with single strokes. (2) Refer to Roll Chart and "Stroke-Bounce" each sixteenth note. (3) Play the quarter and eighth notes louder than the sixteenth notes. (Accent) (4) Alternate the starting hand.

A Rest may be substituted for any note. The counting remains the same. All or part of each section may be played together.

Sixteenth Notes In 2/4 Time

On The 1st And 2nd Beats

(A) Write the counts under the notes. (B) Play.

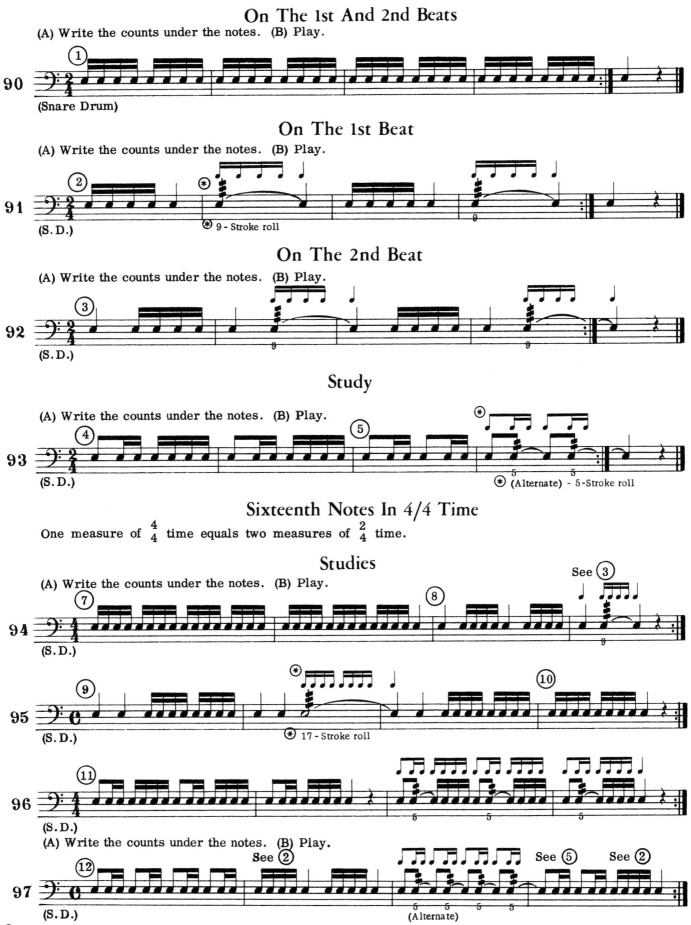

On The 1st Beat

(A) Write the counts under the notes. (B) Play.

On The 2nd Beat

(A) Write the counts under the notes. (B) Play.

Study

(A) Write the counts under the notes. (B) Play.

Sixteenth Notes In 4/4 Time

One measure of $\frac{4}{4}$ time equals two measures of $\frac{2}{4}$ time.

Studies

(A) Write the counts under the notes. (B) Play.

(A) Write the counts under the notes. (B) Play.

✳ The student who is unable to develop a good roll, may divide the notes designated as rolls into sixteenth notes and play with single strokes.

Drums

Sixteenth Notes In 3/4 Time
Studies

(A) Write the counts under the notes. (B) Play.

Sixteenth Notes With Eighth Notes
Studies In 2/4 Time

(A) Write the counts under the notes. (B) Play.

Staccato Etude

Arban (adapted)

Study

(A) Write the counts under the notes. (B) Play.

Etude

Arban (adapted)

Rakes Of Mallow

Irish Folk Tune

Duet
American Patrol

Meacham

Studies In 4/4 Time

(A) Write the counts under the notes. (B) Play.

Jan - U - A - Ry Feb-Ru - A - Ry Sun - Day Mon - Day

(S.D.) 1 e & a 2 e & a 3 & 4 &

Sun-Day Mon-Day Jan-U-A-Ry Sun-Day

(S.D.) 1 & 2 & 3 e & a 4 &

Etude

See Study 100

(Flamacue)

Drums

Scale Studies

(A) Write the counts under the notes. (B) Play.

Duet
A Grotesque Dance

Allegro   17th Century Dance

Studies In 3/4 Time

(A) Write the counts under the notes. (B) Play.

Duet
Folk Dance

Danish

116 Moderato

S.D.
B.D.

mp

Fine *mf*

D.C. al Fine

The Dotted Eighth Note
Rhythm Chart

117 (A) Chorale read – Tap foot. (B) Count and clap – Tap foot. (C) Play – Tap foot.

Jan-U-A-Ry Feb-Ru-A-Ry Jan-U-A-Ry Feb-Ru-A-Ry

Jan-U-A-Ry Feb-Ru-A-Ry

Jan-U-A-Ry Feb-Ru-A-Ry Jan-U-A-Ry

x   y   z

1 e & a   2   e & a   3 e & a   4   e & a

1   & a   2   & a   3   & a   4   & a

1 &   a 2 &   a 3 &   a 4 &   a

This rhythm may also be
associated with the words –

Day   to Day   to Day, etc.

Emphasis is placed on "Day".
Count: 1 – a – 2 – a – etc.

Studies

(A) Write the counts under the notes. (B) Play.

118

(Snare Drum)

119

(S.D.)

120

(S.D.)

Drums

Duet
Battle Hymn Of The Republic

Howe

Duet
Joy To The World

Handel

Harmony And Rhythm
Oh, Faithful Pine

Hohman

Processional

Maestoso

H.W.R.

✹ Bass Drum and Cymbal together.
Drums

Technical Studies
Long Tones

Scale Study

Snare Drum - See Long Roll No. 1 in Roll Chart.

Pares

Burgmuller
(adapted)

Etude

Long Tones

Scale Study

Jancourt

Etude
(Flamacue)

Kohler
(adapted)

Long Tones

Drums

Scale Study

Pares

Chromatics

CHROMATIC means ascending or descending by half steps.

ENHARMONIC TONES are notes that sound and finger the same, but are written on different degrees of the staff and have different names.

Enharmonic Tones

133 Tacet

134 Tacet

Chromatic Scale

135 Tacet

Etude

Czerny
(adapted)

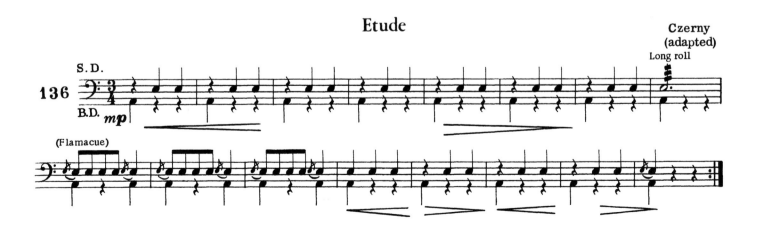

Drums

Duet
Flower of Damascus

Saverio
(adapted)

Moderato

137

S.D.
B.D.
mp

mf

✱ Rinforzando (accent).

Six - Eight Rhythm

138 In this rhythm, an eighth note is the unit for counting.

6 Six counts in a measure.

8 An eighth note receives one count.

A quarter note - ♩ - receives two counts; a dotted quarter note - ♩. - three counts; a dotted half note ♩.- six counts. Sixteenth notes-♪ or ♫-will receive one half count each. A rest of like value may be substituted for any note without changing the counting.

When counting this rhythm, emphasize counts ONE and FOUR by tapping the foot on these counts: 1 2 3 4 5 6. Practice will develop a feeling for the rhythm of SIX counts to a measure, but only TWO "Beats". Thus in fast tempo the dotted quarter note - ♩. - becomes the unit of a count and "Beat".

Six - Eight Rhythm Chart

139 (A) Count and clap - Tap foot. (B) Play - Tap foot.
Repeat each rhythm many times.

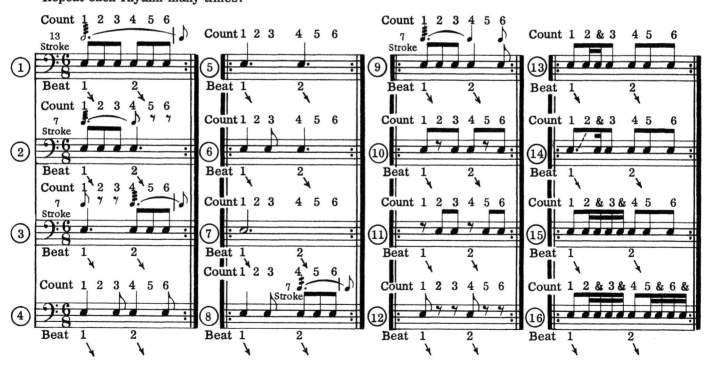

On rhythms designated as the primary strokes for rolls -
  (1) Play the eighth notes with single strokes.
  (2) Refer to Roll Chart and "Stroke-Bounce" each eighth note.
  (3) Alternate the starting hand.

Drums

Six-Eight Time

Practice the following studies counting SIX to a measure. Accent counts ONE and FOUR with a "Beat".

Then review all studies counting and beating TWO to a measure. The dotted quarter note (♩.) will become the unit of a count and "Beat".

Studies

(A) Write the counts under the notes. (B) Play.

Humpty - Dumpty

Rig-A-Jig-Jig

Studies

(A) Write the counts under the notes. (B) Play.

✲ The student who is unable to develop a good roll, may divide the notes designated as rolls into eighth notes and play as single strokes.

Drums

Hunters Song

Folk Tune

Scale

149 Tacet

Study

(A) Write the counts under the notes and rests. (B) Play.

Farmer In The Dell

Folk Song

Hickory Dickory Dock

Folk Song

Rhythm Tricks - Pop Goes The Weasel

Folk Song

(A) Write the counts under the notes and rests. (B) Play.

Duets
Sailing

Marks

Carnival Of Venice

Folk Song

Drums

Harmony And Rhythm
Scherzino

Le Couppey

Technical Studies
Chromatic Scale

157 Tacet

Studies

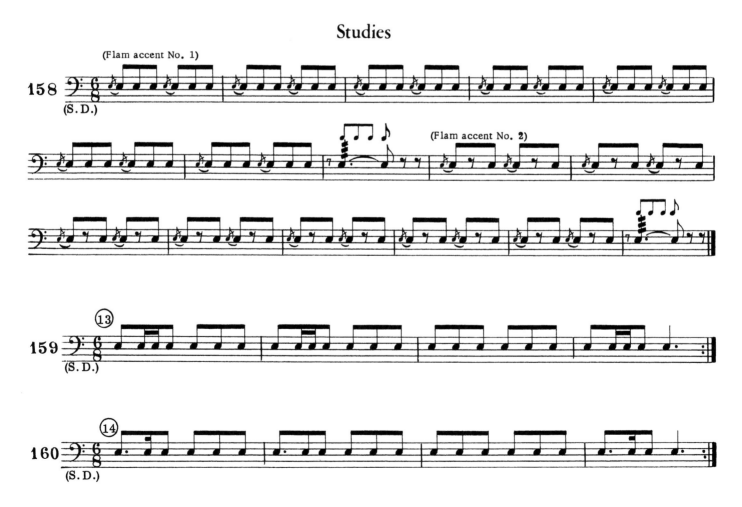

Etude

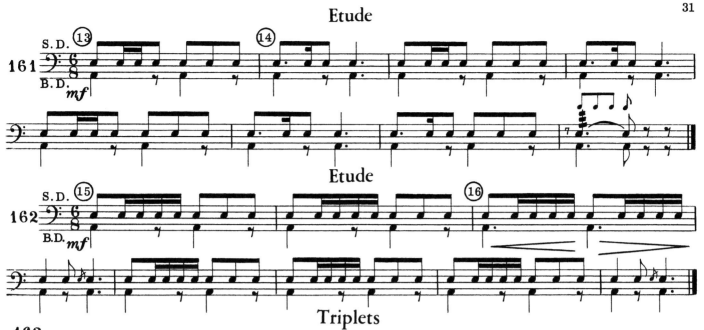

Triplets

163 TRIPLETS are groups of THREE equal notes played in the time of two notes of the same denomination. A triplet of eighth notes - (♪♪♪)is equal in time value to two eighth notes - (♫) or one quarter note (♩).

Triplets are indicated by a number "3" placed over or under a group of notes.

The Rhythm Of Triplets

164 The rhythm of triplets is THREE to the "Beat". Tap the foot in a ONE -↘- TWO -↘- rhythm and associate the word Sa - Tur - Day - Sa - Tur - Day with the "Beats".
Pronounce each syllable distinctly and with equal emphasis - Sa - Tur - Day   Sa - Tur - Day

Count the triplets 1 - & - a, 2 - & - a - - - - - - - - -1 & a 2 & a

Triplet Rhythm Chart

165 (A) Chorale read - Tap foot. (B) Count and clap - Tap foot. (C) Play - Tap foot.
Repeat each rhythm many times.

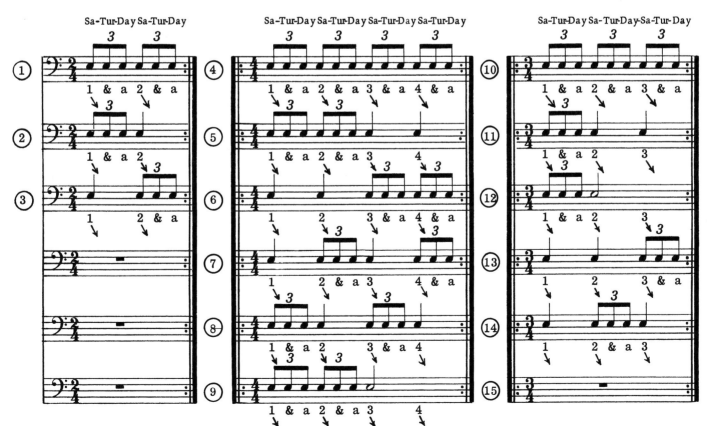

A Rest may be substituted for any note. The counting remains the same.
All or part of each section may be played together.

Drums

Triplets In 2/4 Time
Studies

(A) Write the counts under the notes. (B) Play.

Triplets In 4/4 Time
Studies

(A) Write the counts under the notes. (B) Play.

Etude

Czerny (adapted)

Triplets In 3/4 Time

(A) Write the counts under the notes. (B) Play.

La Gazza Ladra

Rossini

Drums

Duets
Whistling

Triplets And Eighth Notes
Studies

(A) Write the counts under the notes. (B) Play.

Kangaroo Hop

Studies

(A) Write the counts under the notes. (B) Play.

Polka

Harmony And Rhythm
Avalanche

Playing Independent Parts
Row Row Row Your Boat

Drums

Alla Breve Time

186 Alla Breve - $\frac{2}{2}$ -, or Cut Time - ¢ - is played the same as - $\frac{2}{4}$ - time - TWO "Beats" to a measure. However, each note receives half the value that was given it in $\frac{2}{4}$ or $\frac{4}{4}$ time.

A whole note -(o)- receives two counts, a half note (d) - one count, a quarter note -(♩)- 1/2 count, and an eighth note (♪) or (♫) - 1/4 count.

187 The following two lines have the same "Beat" and rhythm. Use the word associations previously learned in $\frac{2}{4}$ time.

Alla Breve Rhythm Chart

188 (A) Chorale read - Tap foot. (B) Count and clap - Tap foot. (C) Play - Tap foot. Repeat each rhythm many times.

The rhythm -

♩. ♪ ♩. ♪

may also be associated with the words -

Day   to Day   to Day, etc.
Count 1 - a - 2 - a - etc.

⊛ To Chorale read the quarter notes in ¢ time. (Eighth notes in $\frac{2}{4}$ time.)

A Rest may be substituted for any note. The counting remains the same.
All or part of each section may be played together.
⑧ ⑨ ⑩ ⑪ ⑫ ⑬ - Primary strokes for designated rolls. First play the eighth notes with single strokes. Refer to Roll Chart and "Stroke-Bounce" eighth note.

Drums

Studies

The Tie In Alla Breve Time

Studies

Sharpshooters March

Drums

Rests In Alla Breve Time
Studies
(A) Write the counts under the notes and rests. (B) Play.

The Dotted Half Note In Alla Breve Time
Study

(A) Write the counts under the notes. (B) Play.

Eighth Notes In AllaBreve Time
Studies

(A) Write the counts under the notes. (B) Play.

✱The student who is unable to develop a good roll, may divide the notes designated as rolls into eighth notes and play with single strokes.

Drums

Duet
She'll Be Comin' Round The Mountain

Folk Song

Harmony And Rhythm
Blue Bells Of Scotland

Melody And Accompaniment
Stars And Stripes Forever

(S.D.) If necessary divide the notes designated as rolls into eighth notes.

Drums

Syncopation

214 Syncopation introduces notes on the unaccented "Beat"; or off the "Beat" entirely. The notes are carried past the next "Beat" where the accent would normally fall. To better understand a syncopated figure, divide the measure into notes of the smallest denomination in the measure. Write in the counts and then tie the notes together that will produce the syncopated rhythm. Refer to the Rhythm Chart.

Syncopation Rhythm Chart

215 (A) Compare the two lines. (B) Count and clap - Tap foot. (C) Play - Tap foot. Repeat each rhythm many times.

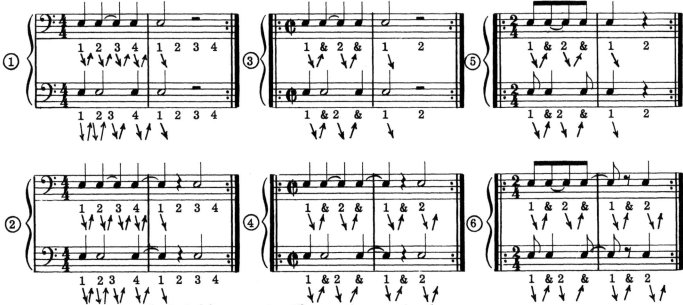

A Rest may be substituted for any note. The counting remains the same. All or part of each section may be played together.

Syncopation In 4/4 And ₵ Time
Study

(A) Write the counts under the notes and rests. (B) Play.

216

Etude

217

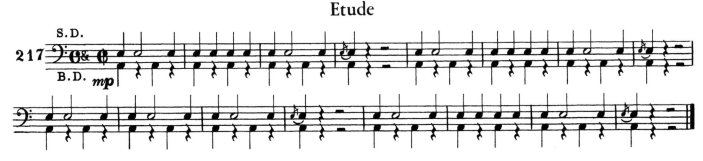

Drums

Our Boys Will Shine
College Song

Study
(A) Write the counts under the notes and rests. (B) Play.

John Henry
Work Song (adapted)

Syncopation In 2/4 Time
Study
(A) Write the counts under the notes and rests. (B) Play.

Etude

The Old Gray Mare
Folk Song

⊛ Check the kind of roll to be used. In C-time use a 17 stroke roll. In ¢ - a 9-stroke roll, etc. Do the same for all of the following studies and songs.
⊛⊛ Check the roll to be used.
Drums

Study

(A) Write the counts under the notes. (B) Play.

Dese Bones

Folk Song (adapted)

Duet
The Caissons Go Rolling Along

Gruber

Harmony And Rhythm
L'il Liza Jane

Lachau

Dance Song

Czech

✸ Check the roll to be used.

Drums

229 to **240** - Tacet -
Review rolls and rudiments

241 to **252** - Tacet -
Review rolls and rudiments